HUMAN NATURE

—◈◈—

~ A Collection of Poems ~

Larry Foster

HUMAN NATURE

A Collection of Poems

Copyright © 2020 Larry Foster

Printed in the United States of America

ISBN# 978-0-9644205-7-1

Library of Congress Control Number: 2020906054

Cover Art: Erycka Cabera

Cover Design: Roel Sanchez

Contributing Artist: Kailey Fregd, Tanna Fiorentino

Contributing Editors: Vanessa Marie Gonzalez

Contributing Writer: Yinju Lin

Published by Books by Anthony Parnell

DEDICATION

III-III-XCIV

The blueprints to a black heart created this timeless masterpiece. I dedicate this to the one that represents the past, the future and the present. Whatever we leave behind and whatever is yet to come, just know my words will heal.

INTRODUCTION

Human nature is a bundle of characteristics, including ways of thinking, feeling, and acting, which humans are said to naturally possess. Our essence between life and death are depicted by our lifetime. Time, only existing to give humans a sense of purpose and to keep track of our progression here on earth.

Though we are the only species bound to time, if we all disappeared, life on earth would still exist and evolve. It is in our nature to record our history through languages created to communicate emotions, but not necessarily define them. General terms are used to justify our actions based on random human desires but not truly a representation of a humanity's intent.

After much contemplation, I decided to write about the one question that agitates me as a writer. Is my perception of the truth reality? Do the laws that bind me to morals and ethics even have a merit for existence?

I live on a planet that is divided into nations with various beliefs of creation, the afterlife, societal norms, and basic human rights. I can go on forever. We create alternate realities through motion picture storylines, gaming software, virtual reality, and yet we dismiss the truth of what is fact.

How does one become intelligent in a society that keeps secrets from the masses? How can you be sure that the words that you speak aren't the misspoken renditions of misguided lies you have been taught?

Science and education are forever evolving. So, does that mean that there are generations that have been exposed to the truth? Or, are there generations that have been exposed to what was thought to be factual?

While writing this book, I decided to study extensively on the make-up society. I researched topics such as Law, Science, Medicine, Technology, Religion and Literature in an effort to cultivate the collective truth. In this quest for knowledge, I gained insight into numerous inconsistencies and abnormalities within and between these disciplines. I found ill intent as well as genuinely good intentions in each of these institutions of our society.

This work of literature also looks at the human mind and the components that make it whole. The outlook is one of how chronic pain affects the mind perspective of how it sees itself. It also explores different aspects of our body and how we have evolved over time to make improvements to ourselves: how over time diseases and injuries have required us to seek out cures and the improvement of the quality of life.

A house without walls lacks the necessary defense for its inhabitants to thrive. So, I invite you to join me on my search for self-discovery in a reality where truth and fact are synonyms with different meanings. Let us research the makeup of our sole protector.

Please understand that perception does not have a one size fits all approach. We are all humans. Nothing more, nothing less. Thus, this written material was not created for one concept to be embraced but for the reader to grasp their own feelings while reading and knowing the context of what inspired this work.

Larry Foster

PRELUDE

Sixth Sense

A poetic premonition to an endless deja vu
that was always meant to be.
The vainness of twenty-twenty vision in lo of a
flawed society.
My intellect is childproof,
I refute a puerile state of mind.

I will never sympathize with deceit or comprehend
mutiny.
Doubt began to seep into my perception.
The vibe was all wrong, so I refinanced my flow.
I'm a horrible judge of character in search of
prosperity.
I only see people as assets and liabilities;
however, they are all temporary.

My ambitions make me shallow.
I'm unsympathetic.
The Blueprints to a Black Heart showed me my
emotions were too deep.
So, I refocused my flow to mirror *Poetic Serenity*.
I envisioned anarchy and the essence of past
visionaries.
A *Timeless* rendition of past, present and future.
The poetic gift that keeps on giving, insight to
life's contextual deja vu.

CONTENTS

Letter of Intent

———⋅⟨⊰⋅⊱⟩⋅———

To whom it may concern,

The place where I laid my head, isn't where you
rested your soul.
The eminent domain to our own well-being.
I write to you in search of self-identity.
An illiterate soul with rhetoric meant to outlast.

Words used to define uncertainty.
Watch my words influence a society designed to
manipulate.
Propaganda meant to sway the youth.
My attempt to diminish the mortality rate.
I only desire to put the wisdom back in your
tooth.
Freestyle poetry as I innovate poetic serenity.
Literacy, the one true accomplice to the truth.
Libel, the only opposition to soul literacy.
Healing through writing, the logical approach to
reasoning.

THE SEASON OF I

I was tired from my dreams, yet they were the
only thing that kept me awake.
I was the common denominator to the potential
that lay dormant to my ambitions.
Scars left me scared of being scarred.
However, I was not scared of the scares that will
leave me scarred.

Where's the purity in the puerile of being
introduced to puberty?
The childhood behind the man.
What time will be my history?
I stopped living by the words of those who came
before.

I was losing my vision,
So, I had to envision a twenty-twenty point of
view.
I only needed me to justify me.
Quality over quantity would always be the
standard.
Deja vu would be the remedy to my poetic
serenity

You knew me
I would always roleplay to let the wordplay get the
best of me.

In your absence, never truly reaching my full
potential.
Because you were the rest of me
I brought out the worst in you to appreciate the
best of me.
Yet you always remind me of the best in me
You knew me well enough to lead me to well only
to wish me well.

For the current me to deny you
would be like a butterfly denying the larva that
created the caterpillar.
However, these times cause for precaution
So, just the thought of you will suffice.

Through thick and thin,
You could see through the thin line between
the lines of my deception and my affection.
Soul over reality was our golden rule.
We were part of a whole
Yet we disregarded the humanity in inhumane.

I only existed outside your expectations except
when we accepted reality.
I didn't mean to materialize our love,
I just wanted the expectations to materialize.

You stopped expecting the world from me.
Poetry became my audience to serenity.
I sought to put our history in its place.
I get tired of you.
Now my rhyme is the rhythm of our blues
Knowing you will always come back to this Deja
vu.

The Opening Act

My subconscious regained consciousness.
So, I took out a pen and began to write again.
I wrote it all down in one sitting.
I remember seeing my thoughts on paper for the
first time.
My subconsciousness just couldn't relate.
It awakened a self-perception of myself that was
foreign to my anatomy.
I read the words out loud as my subconscious
read along.
The words revealed an endless as ja vu.
I began to ponder the passion behind the pain.
Rhetoric of a soul in agony.
Were these words written for me or were they
written for you?
Regardless of the intended audience, they became
reality.
As soon as my pen touched the paper, an endless
rhyme took control.
Thus, began my search for poetic serenity.

TWENTY-FIVE

———⋅◈⋅———

This is where he finds his balance.
A puerile mindset with adult tendencies.
This is where his story becomes history to tell.
This is where he reveals the childhood behind the
man.
The blueprints out of his hell.
A quarter of life deferred.
Death was a liability, so he invested his assets
into reality.
A quarter of a century
let the story begin at five squared.
Healing through writing.
A foreign concept to most,
but to him this was his answer to his story.

MIND GAMES

My soul is my secret ghostwriter.
It tends to write from a third person point of view.
A blank canvas comes to life.
Words seemingly create a deliberate Deja vu.
I wasn't born of sin, yet I live in repentance.
Death is the cost of living.
How ominous, we all live differently, yet we live
out the same life sentence.

A mindset that is never without the knowledge of
reality.
Would your soul speak its mind?
If your subconscious didn't lead you astray?
Time after time,
I wonder what your soul would have to say.

Would my soul still be desirable if it was pure?
And couldn't relate to your pain?
An intellect racist ahead of his time.
Would you still open the book if you didn't like
the cover?
If I told you the truth was in healing through
writing.
Would you believe in soul literacy, in search of
serenity?

You adored everything I hated about me.
Writing to you has made me less like me and
more like you.

My favorite poem was the one where I would write
your name repeatedly
Not out of love, but to sketch out our history.
You used to tell me that I was crazy and
abnormal beyond belief.
I didn't mind letting my guard down because I
had built up my foundation.

Your bark was your bite.
That's how I know you wouldn't be enough to
appease my appetite.
I would've been yours in a heartbeat, but I don't
think you keep up with the pace
I would listen, but it wasn't until your departure
that I heard your pleas.
I moved away to put distance between insanity.
I just didn't factor the mental strain it would put
on my sanity.

WORDS FROM THE WELL

While in pursuit of happiness,
did you ever consider that you were running away
from agony?
For those who must live in pain daily,
remember to pat yourself on the back.
You're stronger than you think you are.
Without people like you, passion would have no
grit.

You are your own brand.
Surround yourself with progress.
Never be complacent or stagnate.
Be intentional and transparent in your thoughts,
feelings, and motives.
Higher expectations output a higher quality of
life.

You're more successful and valuable than you
think.
Keep yourself. Keep moving forward.
Keep breaking barriers.
Most of all, keep believing that your dreams...
will become a memory in your reality.

ALLURE

---·❦·---

Let it be in your stride.
Let it become your voice.
Walk with authority, but never too tall to bow to
grace.

Let it be in your rhetoric.
Let it become your presence.
Speak with clarity, but never too pretentious to
listen.

Let it be in your style.
Let it become your brand.
Dress sharp, but consider the company you
wish to attract.

Let it be in your art.
Let it become your truth.
Create with a blank canvas, but never open your
mind to pessimism.

Live deliberately.
In every aspect of your reality.
Live like it's golden.

THE ESSENTIALS

Take only what you want.
On this journey, you will discover what you
desire.
Based on your belief my words may reaffirm
Faith.
Take only what you desire.
On this journey, you will discover what you have.
Based on your faith my words may reaffirm
Grace.
Take only what you have.
On this journey, you will discover what is meant.
Based on your grace my words may reaffirm
Logic.
Take only what you need.
On this journey, you will discover what is to be.
Based on your logic my words may reaffirm
Love.
On this journey, you will discover what could be.
Based on your love my words may reaffirm
Hope.
Bring these things only.
On this journey for the essentials for healing.

PARDON

My love for you is infinite, I will always be able to
look past our history.
I'm bound to you; time has become the backstory
to our Deja vu.
I am incapable of harboring hate towards you
despite the afflictions of our past.
We live to die, while the dead rest in peace with
no will to live.
Readers become the protagonist of a writer's
autobiography.
I pity your twenty-twenty vision; a blink of an eye
doesn't even reveal the rest of me.
My crazy is starting to get crazy, even my
monologues have become self-aware.
Even when I take a step forward, my past seems
to be a step ahead of me.
I'll die thinking of you, but I won't live blind in
lieu of our Deja vu.
Tell me how you feel when you're around me.
So, we never have to reminisce about how we
used to be.
It's my dying wish, that through my will, you'll
look past our history.

NOMADIC LUST

The complexity of a commitment disorder.
Heads in beds or beds in heads.
Which one was first?
Is that what he or she said?
Come and go as you please.
Never spending too much time on your knees.
Praying for a love meant to last.
Never spending too much time facing down.
Praying for the lust to come to past.
Never spending too much time on your back.
Partners formulated through attrition.
Spreading the word as a missionary.
Amongst the most desirable position.
The inability to be faithful based on bias of truth.
Sexual orientation creates a lackluster of
affection.
Often contemplating the thought of love.
Love habitually clouding the veil of deception.
With the introduction of time maybe a settlement
will be introduced.

READER'S DIGEST

To harbor one's emotions into words is to define
the unknown.
To find peace in words creates a falsehood of
serenity.
In solitude, I would laugh out loud to myself.
Dreams were the antonyms to the life I lived,
while nightmares were the synonyms to the
life I had become accustomed to.
Being reliable meant I was available to myself.
I would have had more friends if listened more
than I spoke,
but then my silence would've carried a heavier
burden when they reached out to me.
I didn't beg, but that didn't mean I didn't desire
change.
My patience had become impatient.
I was beneath forgiveness and forgiving.
A savage to say the least.
In solitude, reflections showed what most had
come with fear.
However, the truth be told there's beauty behind
every beast.

LUCID

———◈◈◈———

Even though you spent the night inside my head.
I awoke to an empty bed.
Thoughts of you clouded my judgement.
As your arms cradled my soul,
thoughts of our past became the narrator of my
nightmares.
Scattered memories of your deception.
A reenactment of our future to a reality that
would never be.
I began to let my imagination take control.
In truth, my mind was controlling me.
I woke to a dream deferred by reality.
The man in the mirror was the cause for the lack
thereof.
His commitment to his commitment disorder
Forever rendering him alone to experience life
and death.
He said nothing could last forever, but their
memories never seemed to fade.
He turned his nightmares into dreams.
And in return he gave himself the essence of
agony.
A constant state of a be or not to be.
How could he have known that in between life
and death, that he would be the muse to his
serenity.

Subconscious Oath

When I awoke from my coma,
I perceived from that of a stillborn.
A blank memory for a blank canvas.
The restoration of my intellectual property.
Regrets erased in search of serenity.
A reset for my emotional intelligence.
In search of a new self-worth.
The reinstatement of morals and values.
A puerile approach to love and lust.
A soul baptized by its own hands.
It was the only way to ensure success.
The reincarnation of a poetic genius.

That which stimulates my mind and shelters my
soul.
Shall we never run from our past but consolidate
our future.
Our pain is as excruciating as the days are
plenty.
Utilizing that pain as we work toward our desire
of internal peace.
We free ourselves from those who cannot forgive us.
In forgiving all the pain others have caused us,
we illuminate ourselves.
Everything we do today is to create a foundation
for a better tomorrow.
Discovering an internal essence within us with
each new phase.

PAIN MATURED

———·❧·❧·———

Breaking up with your first love
as I remember you were my last.
The memory of your pain as you showed me the
same.
I remember how I felt when you told me your
name.
A nerve conditioned to eternity.
That moment defined my well-being.

For years to come, you would shadow my
reflection.
Who knew from that moment on that
with every thought my subconscious would be
tainted.
I've watched you hurt those I love based on
agony.
You showed me internal every lasting pain
And I proceeded to show them the same.
To write to you as I type is to write as I should.
This is the only literature that will heal my soul.

For years you impeded on my ability to
be made whole.
When I spoke, you were my one true voice.
My actions reflected your will.
I can feel you now as I type.
Your unwavering essence glaring out from me as
I write.

For me to let you go would mean to journey to a
time
when I could speak without an undertone of pain.
Where I could think without the thought of your
agony.

This is our end.
A break from a condition that was meant for
eternity.
A makeup of the years I have lost to uncertainty.
I just hope you see that you were the best part of
me.
The part of me that appreciates my love for
serenity.

TIMELESS

A star gaze upon the skies
gravity pulls it to its core.
An endless space full of time.
A distant black whole forevermore.

A mother gazes upon her children,
nature changes seasons.
An endless abundance of life.
A distant future shall stand to reason.

A windows gazes into its home,
furniture seamlessly pushed around.
An endless layout of décor.
A foundation holds its ground.

A fiancé gazes upon her diamond,
carat becomes more precious than gold.
An endless love is understood.
A story just beginning to unfold.

A writer gazes upon his canvas
thoughts become words unknowingly.
An endless rhyme.
A gift blessed by poetry.

REFLECTIVE RHETORIC

———◦⟨⟩◦———

Eloquence for your self-esteem.
Your smile comes from your reflection.
You must learn how to smile back.

Be the Atlas to your own world.
So, when you fall, you will also stand.
Your happiness comes from your perception.
You must see a way out of no way.

Be the foundation of your home.
So, when you fall apart, you have something to
build upon.
Your ambitions come from your dreams.
You must take aim at reality.

Dreams are just your reality deferred.
Expect greatness from yourself.
Karma has taught us what is given, is received.
Being reliable also means being available for your
own personal growth.
Reflect humility and civility, and you will find
serenity.

ONOMATOPOEIA

My hellos are stained with goodbyes.
A glutton for pain.
I'm unplugged running on backed up emotions.
Only seeking despair that engulfs love.
Solitary confinement, my soul's humble abo
My walls are not to keep you out, but to keep it
from you.
The psych awarded me.

Detached from the humility of sympathy.
My emotions derived from an artificial intellect
perspective.
A chemical imbalance in a conformed society.
I found a habit in rehabilitation.
Therapy disguised as poetry.

The voice of the mute soul.
All I have are leftover words.
I don't feel the emotions behind them.
Do writers ever receive love notes or just the
experience to create them?
I rolled the dice and solitude bounced back.
One without the other to have and to hold.
What's the difference between a heartbreak and a
heart attack?

Life, the muse to an agony untold.
Look back at the collateral damage in his history.
Where were you amid his contemplation?
A writing community that lacks poetic serenity.
Manipulation for substance in the form of a
charitable donation.
A free writing workshop, listen to the words of
soul literacy.

OUT OF DARKNESS

Healing through writing
what a foreign concept to natural remedy.
Are you the fact or the truth?
I hate rhyming, but it's become my identity.

These are words written from the soul.
A new age of literature.
I don't doubt your perception,
but you must admit I'm your reflection.

A book written on the premise of healing.
A book written for the struggles.
A book written to heal the willing.

Your mentality was designed to create.
No matter what they say
you're chemically imbalanced.
Who can't relate?

My physical, flawed to death.
The perfect being lives inside.
Watch as I cross fit my way to perfection.

Our emotional truth obligated to perception.
How she saw him
became the author of his reflection.

An endless rhyme scheme,
the perfect Deja vu.
I wrote healing through writing.
I did it to save you.

LIFE AFTER

A butterfly who hasn't bloomed, will never know
she's a butterfly until she blooms.
She will spend her whole life searching for the
love and care of others.
Not realizing her own worth and what she has yet
to offer.
A butterfly that hasn't bloomed
will never know she's beautiful.
She will spend the early part of her life wondering
if she is too short,
is she too fat, is she of worth, is she enough, or if
she will find happiness?
Not realizing that this is only the beginning and
she still is yet to bloom.
A butterfly that hasn't bloomed
will never know the wonders she's meant to see
and the butterfly she's meant to be.
I just hope this butterfly stays long enough to see
not realizing that once she blooms,
as she begins to spread her wings,
She'll be free.

My Majorette

My queen to be.
I'm only a mate born of fate.
My soul tells me to endure.
Serenity says the best is yet to come.
My flow tells me to let go.
I'm only writing because life refuses to free you.
My soulmate says I'm nothing.
Poetry fabricated as aroma therapy.
My agony tells me not to let you go.
I'm only vindictive to prove my love.
My intellect tells me to perceive.
Wisdom spoken behind the veil of shades.
My anatomy says see the world inside out.
I'm only coming around as karma to Deja vu.
My words to you are beyond poetry.
An orchestra without a chorus to sing along.
I am the desire to your serenity
You are the beat to the rhythm in my blues.
I am an enigma to your reality.
When hell confined me to solidarity, you stayed
by me.
I am the content; you are my artistry.
I felt too deep into your heaven.
The final muse to my symphony.

Passive Voice

My right hand was bound to self-destruct.
I was addicted to a low.
My flow was toxic.
Words relinquished aggression.
Overtime, I became your ventriloquist.
Speaking for the reader instead of to.
My rhetoric was intentional.
I had no merit for this discourse.
My belief was solely based on intent
to be my fate's controller.
I was present but lacked a presence.
Justifying my own ramifications
through the most unbecoming of means.
Now that those times have come and gone
all that remains is to change to an active tone.

LESSON LEARNED

Sometimes we're blind to the truth.
The truth about relationships.
The truth about life.
The truth about ourselves.
We can't accept the truth, because ultimately
we come to accept the lie.

The idea of living up to society's expectations.
Doing this, doing that because
they were of accepted norms.
I was blind to who I was as a person
and who I had become.

For years, I was blind to lust.
For years, I was blind to what life meant.
People saw the change in me,
but I looked at my reflection
and saw a recurring agony.

Now, I'm no longer blind to the truth.
No more deceived by relatives that don't relate.
I can see myself for who I am.
No longer accustomed to those lies
I see life through my own eyes.

ACQUITTED

The mistrial to a life sentenced to pain.
A guilty conscience I must vindicate.
A clear respective I must regain.
Calamity must subdue the tremors of my past.
Every word I write becomes the foundation for my
vindication.
My subconscious to be revived at last.
Healing through writing, the voice of
rejuvenation.
Trauma from vicious renditions of memories.
Every step I take becomes the guide to my
emancipation.
Healing in the form of visual remedies.
Every thought becomes the cornerstone to this
declaration.
Words for the physical and the mental.
Healing through writing,
the epilogue to my acquittal.

I

Isolation that created me
Admiration that boasted me
Society that strayed me
Love that blinded me
Betrayal that surrounded me
Despair that confused me
Hate that changed me
Tears that weakened me
Darkness that protected me
Pain that strengthened me
Family that guided me
Success that willed me
Money that tamed me
Morals that defined me
Intellects that empowered me
Destiny that found me
And writing that freed me.

PERFECT V

I can see far beyond 20/20.
I can feel from the inside out.
I can taste the leftovers in your mouth.
I can hear the truth behind your screams.
I can smell the uncertainty in your dreams.

I can sense all these things

Our eyes cannot lie
they give us away.
Your eyes display life as your mind perceives it.
Your eyes believe what they want to see.

They disclose our true feelings.
Our eyes bleed when they're sad.
Our eyes explode when we feel excited.
Glow when we're in love.

One's eyes are the key to our heart

What am I in this world?
A world that has lost all sanity.
A world with no shame.
A world all about winning the game.
A world all about fame.

How I wish I could change my name.
How I wish I could discover life again.

But there comes a time when you must realize.
That through your eyes, that this is reality.
You must begin to listen to yourself.
You must be able to smell the presence of air.
Feel the love of the ones that care.
And not be afraid to taste the unknown.

I just hope perfect vision comes with serenity.

NO SECT

Birth of origins defining men.
An infinitive universe both vast and puerile.
The cultural influence of their region.
Creating faiths that transcend time and reason.
The constant exploration into our past.
Each religion birthed through manipulation.
Fabricated lies into the form of faith.
Passed down generation after generation.
Spreading their word based on fate.
The authors of peace become the terror of hate.
How many innocents throughout the test of time
by sword or conversion
have been victims of a religious crime?
An atheist, Hindu and Judaism teachings,
Christian Crusaders and an Islamic State.
What if they were the source of all hate?
The complexity of finding the answer to life.
What if the world came together in a cohesive
speech?
And not based on how far their God can reach.
What if instead of falling to our knees praying out
to space,
we looked internally for our peace, love and
grace?

Temptress Allure

———— ⋅❦⋅ ————

Once upon a time a soul had a mate.
One as synonymous as the sky was blue.
Life set sail on the conquest to discover their
truth.
His bow was her alpha.
Her stern was his Omega.
She called out to him as the
sea yearned for his love.
He was the passion to her pain.
Her tears were life's mental strain.
One without the other.
To have and to hold.
With no compass to lead him astray.
Under the veil of love,
her love would show him the way.
She would become his Odyssey.
A lighthouse beckoning his soul to shore.
She would become his muse.
A treasure with no trove.
She would become his fantasy.
He reminded her of a soul she once knew.
For a siren's appeal,
was a rendezvous with Deja vu.
Til death do they part,
fate was their I do.

To have and to Hold

It's my business, it's my flow.
Watch me rhythm watch me blues.
The spoken session to the truth.
This paper is my booth.
Introduce you to a Deja vu.
The sweetest love, my rendezvous.

His hands were the backbone to my truth.
As we swayed his business became my flow.
It was his style; it was his grace.
The alpha to my omega.
His vibe began to erase.

The depth of your affection gave me hope.
As you slid into this rhyme with a heavy stroke.
Just knowing your aching soul.
Would cling to every word that I wrote.

Her lust showed no veil.
The passion to her pain became sex appeal.
We became entrapped in our insanity.
With every stroke, my soul began to yearn for
you.

I say watch me rhythm, I say watch me blues.
Spoken word is the new Deja vu.
You see the truth of the matter
is that this is my rhyme.

The ability to switch genders is my sign.
The visuals on replay.
Turn up the bass in my booth.
The sweetest love, my rendezvous.

Welcome to the essence of bisexuality.
One without the other
to have and to hold.
The stringent love affair between the two.
A ménage à trois
The only scenario where I say I do.

THE SUNNY TRUTH

This is your covenant to peace, honor and justice.
A beautiful story will unfold.
One where you will find your peace.
For the burdens of your affection
will transform into perfection.
I hear the pain in your tears.
You are the perfect addition to this endless Deja
vu.
I see you standing on your will.
An imperfect utopia lies beneath the thought of
you
As you honor him by carrying for his legacy.
Shedding your soul ever so often.
Becoming one with liberty.
The prelude to a perfect scene.
Time becoming your justice.
I see the beauty in your essence.
The reason the sun rises in the east.
I feel a soul so radiant.
The thought of you as I release.
A writer's muse.
These are the words that I confess.
In life, you are my reality.

PERSPECTIVE

———— ⋅⟨⟩⋅ ————

I'm introverted to my depression.
I'm incapable of seeing my reflection in the
mirror.
I'm inhumane toward my own happiness.
I'm incompatible with my soul mate.
I'm infatuated with my past failures.
I'm inferior to the humans who are not me.
I'm imperfect to society's thoughts of who I
should be.

But then I gained insight to my own truth.
What if my parallels were also obtainable?
How could I implement self-deception?
Would it go a little something like this...?

I'm an extrovert who doesn't mind being alone at
peace.
I'm capable of seeing how others perceive me.
I'm humility with a side of civility.
I'm compatible with the love inside me.
I'm infatuated with the success of my future.
I'm above the human I used to be.
I'm perfect because of my individuality.

IN MY MIND

Let's take a sneak peek
into the magnificent world of insanity.
A psychological encyclopedia.
An index full of illogical reasoning.
Take my hand on this odyssey
into the history of this endless rhyme.
The rhetorical Virgo of astrology.

A perception sure to offend.
An intellectual racist.
Forever charming till the end.
An architectural masterpiece.
A heightened sense of self-worth.
A suave approach to human nature

Their bi-curious approach to intimacy.
Here within lies a disturbed temple.
A constant struggle of life and death.
A tainted neurological pathway.
Namaste has no salutation here.
Remember this is just a peak.
For a full subconscious rendering
would leave most lying at my feet.

The constant need of mental stimulation.
Solitude, my present fear.
A mind bound to contemplation
as the end of this rhyme draws near.

The ability to relate.
A persona personalized to manipulate.
As one's personality comes to fruition.
Even with a twenty-twenty advantage
I often fear that mine is overdue.

As the credits begin to roll
to my reader to which I console.
Know that a sneak peek into my mind
was an undesirable sighting.
Know that a sneak peek into my mind
created the desire of healing through writing.

A WRITER'S CODA

I rolled the dice
and fate bounced back at me.
Your words should tread lightly.
At some point every human will be walked upon.
Death, the thought of emancipation shuns.

I put the cure at our fingers.
Verbal renditions of the past.
Such a double standard our context tends to
show.
We referred to it as healing through writing,
but we wrote in the darkness.

I put my fears at the tip of your fingers.
As I proceed to write
I focused not on the readability,
but on the other context to be imagined.
They were my fears
to be misunderstood by my peers.

I placed your dreams at my fingertips.
I didn't care if the words made sense.
They weren't our reality.
That's the beauty of imaginability.
My subconscious efforts to gain your trust.

I placed the truth at fingers length.
Letters formulating defined tendencies.
A poet meant to educate.
Never trusting his own teachings.
Out of darkness,
the nature of humanity.
A life born seemingly out of fear of being free.

A MUSE

Discern my words, as you incite art.
Hear my plea, as your words sway literature.
Caress my soul, as we mold masterpieces.
Relish our future, as we envision our past.
I write to tell stories meant to last,
I write to keep my sanity,
I wrote my first poem to heal my pain,
I wrote to give a silent soul a stage,
I wrote mostly in a drunken rage,
I wrote so you would hear me
and free me from my cage.

Though we use words to communicate,
oftentimes we speak from within.
We talk where no one can hear us.
Your voice calms me, while my silence bothers
you.
Our presence comforts. Belonging to one another.
Our souls blind to a time where we exist
independently.
A muse to a masterpiece.

You give me warmth where I need it most.
You were the hug I felt from inside the womb.
You are my atlas when I can't stand on my own.
You are my rhythm when I get the blues.
You begin to flow, when I need to let go.
An addiction that takes you higher,

I'm powerless towards the desire.
As definite as any tattoo and greater than any
sexual desire.
More stimulating than any dope, any instinctive
emotion,
and as sure as any faith.
Our love accepts one another.

MIRAGE

I was caught up in disbelief
yet I was living in my reality.
I let the blinders control my perception
yet I was blindsided by my own deception.
I ignored the rumors because I knew the truth.

It wasn't enough to have perfect vision.
I envisioned an alternative universe to counteract
perception.
Manipulating my rhetoric
I swayed public opinion.
Confessions of a liar was the end to my
blueprints.
I witnessed the truth, but my depositions were
nothing but.

The negative feedback became their talking
points.
Yet, I yielded no forum for suggestions.
Stubborn and selfish both adjectives of the blind.
Refusing to see through the eyes of others.
Isolation will be my end.
Maybe my mentality deflects my reality.
While my life bore witness to the opposite of loyalty,
could it be my soul was bound to infidelity?

Leaving me blind to the darkness that I had come
to be.
An inability to filter out the hallucinations.
While I slept, visions haunted me.
Figments of my imagination.

In the distance, I saw my soul reach out to me.
Writing to myself, I saw a life of solitude in the
clear.
My greatest fear is not to see reality.
It's that in my quest for serenity,
I will realize that it was I who healed me.

Signs of Peace

A peace sign is the equivalence to literary
serenity.
Achieve moderation to all your desires and you
will discover internal harmony.
All that is meant will come to be.
The feelings as your worst days come to past.
Let faith be your foundation built to outlast.
Nobody ever has the intent to apologize,
but forgiveness is always necessary.
However unconventional the method maybe,
set aside time to rearrange the thoughts bearing
down on your mind.
Whether it's the conflict of uncertainties
or the author of your desires.
Your essence deviates from the atmosphere in
which you surround yourself.
Waste no time on repetitive rendezvous.
Allow for new outcomes to change the past.
Do these things and have faith in the power of
you.
I'm in love with human nature.
Serenity, the new Deja vu.

SEEK

I thought she was the one to rise.
She thought I was the one to set.
I am her shadow in the sun.
Under the moon, she is my silhouette.

All the while we rotated around our truth.
These lyrics get deeper the farther I am from you.
We found each other in darkness.
We hid in plain view.
These lyrics get deeper the closer I get to you.

She found him face to face searching forevermore.
He found her face to face with a rendezvous.
They dug until they found each other at the
epicenter of their core.
Worlds apart, these lyrics got deeper as we
became Deja vu.

OLIVE BRANCHES

Let's call it even.
Let's call for a truce.
A brand-new season.
Let's not forget our past
but let our efforts be for that reason.
The white flag to the old Deja vu.

Let's let go of finding never.
Let's see past cruel intentions.
Let's be each other's aroma therapy.
A brand new once upon a time.
These are the blueprints to the serenity of my
poetry.
We were lost in the essence of an endless rhyme.

Let's take our memories off replay.
Let's break apart from this endless circle.
Let's wonder about life after forgiveness.
A brand-new rhyme scheme.
In my mind, memories of us, a gift and a curse.

Let's transition from old to new.
Let's make peace, I'm bound to you.
A brand new close enough.
You were the devil of my devil.
The checkmate to the war inside my soul.

Let's put our trilogy on repeat.
Let's come face to face.
Let's let our mind, body, and soul be bound to
a brand new forevermore.
You took me out of darkness.
The closer we get
a lifetime glance becomes our overture.

Let's not forget the lessons learned.
I'm powerless, you are my muse.
To have and to hold.
A brand-new Deja vu.
Healing through writing, it saved me.
I just hope it's enough for me and you.

COLLATERAL BEAUTY

My life was frightening, it was so chaotic.
Full of tunnel visions of my insecurities
I perceived life as a childhood memory.
How could I express the pain that was killing me?
I desired to awake to sure uncertainty.
I created insanity for my enjoyment.
I was lost and forgotten
so much that I've lost my belief.

Now I witness the present through artistry.
Now I awake to beauty.
I'm running towards you.
I'm running away from my insecurities.
Can you hear me?
Because I can envision you.

I've become so free of free will.
I only care about my creativity.
I'm infatuated with this domestic marriage.
With my own understanding.
I love this melody.
It tells me that I'm not crazy.
I begin to get infatuated with my dreams.
I'm just trying to improve my individuality.
I just want life's independency.
I need no one to bear my name.
None to dictate my way of living.

The only collateral I offer is the commodity of free.
You don't have to understand me.
I love to be lonely.
My unwavering desire to live in solitude.
No one should analyze me.
They'll never understand what it is.
What it is to have serenity.

SEASONED CULMINATION

Open season to an open flow.
When leaves fall the trees still stand.
I lose consciousness as they seemingly come and
go.
Winter wonderland to your dreams.
How I wonder what they mean.

Spring has a funny way of letting go.
Summer time love on replay.
Time will move forward,
as you allow the present to grow.
Open seasons lead the way.

Heed my word let the story begin.
Out of darkness,
I was a child born of sin.
Words left unsaid became my pen.
Blueprints to a black heart became my evangelist.
What the future holds lies within history.

I hope you understood this mental approach.
I hope you felt the emotions I wrote.
I hope you found your spiritual truth.
I hope you balance your physical scale.

A life of solitude as I await my fate.
A life of balance as I become my addiction.
A life of mute as I speak from within.
A life of peace as I breathe humility.

As I progress back into myself
I thank you for reading along.
I wrote you a story meant to last.
I finally found an end to this endless rhyme.
An endless Deja vu has come to past.
Who knew healing through writing would come
with time?

RITE OF PASSAGE

Dreams, antonyms to the life I live,
While nightmares become the synonyms, I've
become accustomed to.
What if the heaven I created was just to justify
the hell I created?
Half full...half empty... or maybe the glass was
whole?
When I would hurt you, was it weird that I
wished I was the person you leaned on?
An addiction that connected me to the world.
Once taken away, it left me stranded at its core.
To become an addict to your addiction.
If I took your advice to give up all my vices in
exchange for your love.
Would that exonerate me from my past
afflictions?

I will push and pull you away from your core.
The constant test of the scales of lust and just.
I believe my truth, but the facts are
misconstrued.
My mind daydreams of alternate realities.
I am the liaison between the previous and the
prospective.
Only in pain do I experience stability.
I suppress my emotions in search of balance.
My composure is constant.
I will forever seek out the equivalent to serenity.

The manifest destiny of a narcissistic.
The revival of solitude.
Calculated thoughts in response to selfish
ambitions.
This is a proclamation of civil war.
A one-on-one confrontation with my reflection.
The relief from my mental state.
A departure from unlike minds.
The un-falsified personification of my soul.
My desires return to that which is beautiful and
inherently shallow.
The reestablishment of quality over quantity.
No longer bound to earthly concessions.
I reunite with codependency.

YANG TO YIN

———— ❦ ————

Discovering the unknown that you thought never
existed, exists.
Roaming conversations, a scary feeling of
uncertainty.
To let someone, see through you without
resistance.
On this day, in you I found the silver lining.
Why is karma so amusing?
Even though there's a chance we might be
using....
Each other's soul and insecurity.
Even so, we should embrace it.
Bringing fruition to our coexistence.
The best part of me never meant to be discovered.
Acting as the exact opposite to the insecurities
within me.
Her insanity comforts my soul.
My manhood desires the depths of her mind,
body and spirit.
The literature to my lecture.
Questioning the logic that has blinded me since
birth.
Why does her voice mimic an all to unfamiliar
Deja vu?
Her words read as if they were written by me.
I see your truth as I begin to embrace our
essence.

ABSTRACT

Life blessed me with footnotes
to guide me toward the index of knowledge.
My only regret is that within my writing
Lies a synopsis that will never be lived.

These chapters were written
more often than perceived.
Words underwritten for the final edit by the
reader.
An epilogue bound to its misconception.
Artistry catered toward a healing through writing
outlook.

Poetry based around soul searching
through emotional, spiritual, sexual, mental, and
physical wellness.
This book is to act as a tool that will
elevate our understanding of our connection to
life,
and the emotions-turmoil we are exposed to.

Please understand that perception
does not have a one size fits all approach.
The written material was not created for one
concept to be perceived,
but for the reader to grasp their own feelings
while reading the context.

Reasonable Doubt

Would you still read my content if you didn't like
the cover?
An illiterate soul with a speech impediment.
What's visibly appealing to most might be
intangible to others.
I'm becoming a feign to the abnormalities in
conformity.

When did you forsake yourself?
Was it around the time you forgave yourself?
Your agony is nothing more than research for
soul literacy.
My love is cruel, but my intentions are beautiful.
I'll make you love to ensure one day you hate.
I embody lust. Don't get bodied by sex appeal.
I'm not your probability.
Yet, I do depend on certain outcomes.

So, shallow yet so deep.
Let me rest in peace.
There's an imperfect version of you in my dreams.
There's a perfect version of you in my nightmares.
Life has a habit of showing me the veil between
life and death.

Mind Control

We created literature to persuade our future
souls to conform
Now they lay as a time capsule to our truth
For the time being, your absence is warranted.
My wordplay doesn't faze you.
And my actions would just warrant conflict.
Being understood by you was life's gift to the
most misunderstood.
Yet reality holds you at bay.
Your absence signifies my incompatibility with
humanity.

I had to learn that the world doesn't end
when you can't find your means to an end.
Focused on lust and material gain.
My burdens weighed heavy on stepping stones.
While logic kept me in place,
their incompetence blundered the truth.
The current me is content with I.
I was overzealous to approach life with common
sense.
In hindsight, solitude was the only way we would
see eye to eye.

Restricted Access

My hellos were stained with goodbyes.
I was unplugged running on backup emotions
Only seeking despair that engulfs love.
The front door was always open; however,
The back door was more appealing.
I was trespassing on private property.
Yet you gave me the master key to your soul.
The lies made for a prettier truth.
Our deceit becomes second nature.
The truth was always meant to be.

Solitary confinement was my souls' humble
abode
My walls were not to keep you out, but to keep it
from you
Detached from the humility of sympathy
My emotions were derived from an artificial
intellect perspective
A chemical imbalance in a conformed society
The psych ward awarded me
I found a habit in rehabilitation
Therapy in the form of poetry

TRAIL OF TEARS

———◄3•℈►———

Until death do us part, a soulmate's anguish.
A covenant to a soul's desire to be revived as a
whole.
The odyssey to the nonexistence reality in which
they coexist.
To give up on you is to ignore our past lives and
those yet to be lived.
My only hope rests solely on the embryo of our
love to reunite us with grace.
Utopian ambitions, in your solidity, I only yearn
to rest in peace.

Time after time, fate proved that our essence
belonged to Deja vu.
Viewer discretion advised.
I wrote a thesis statement to test the theory of
time.
The following content in unsuitable for the weak
hearted,
And virgins alike as well.
I see time as our accomplice to retribution.
Bait, hook, catch, release.
The past present and future that outlines our
history.

You will always return to Deja vu.

MONTAGE

Words meant nothing without the meaning
behind them.
Two poets in love were nothing short of
opposition research.
The sands of time repeat our history
while counting down to our future.
Effort proves the rhetoric in which we chose to
pronounce our love.
Why look forward to our future,
when we have the present to determine our fate.

I was just wet clay in search of a potter.
Molded to manifest a masterpiece.
To be more than a memory,
a solemn swear I do.
I would rather have been the rock of your
foundation
than your mountain's peak.
To outlast your legacy,
a memorial to your will.
Of no relation; however, you were my family.

Some people were content with what they saw,
while others tried to envision the bigger picture.
I just desired to be your canvas.
Though we saw the same thing,
how we perceived reality made us unique.
Two soulmates bound to a masterpiece,

An artist with no muse,
one without the other we became incomplete.

Love and hate become our Deja vu.
As the pendulum swings back and forward,
I write from me to you.
Dear, will always be the prelude to my foreword.
I was sincere when I said I do.
Sincerely, the epilogue to move us forward.
Words become our rendezvous.

,

————— ❖ —————

The separation of a dependent clause from the
independent other.
The departure from our normal routine.
A bite of an apple and a vision of the unforeseen.
Wisdom seemingly separating fate.
A leaf falls while the tree still stands.
Departing from its source of life.
Withering away with no second chance.
Gone with the wind, fate's sacred sacrifice.
The seasons danced with the wind.
On a whim, this lovers quarrel found its end.
Silence will always fall on deaf ears.
De ja vu, let the story begin.

OUT OF FOCUS

———·❦·———

Farewell to my passion
Until we meet again.
Bisexual tendencies, I prefer beauty.
Love comes and goes.
Memories don't have a return policy.

I'm just too beautiful to care anymore.
Currency comes and goes.
I took love out of the equation and inserted
instant gratification.
I'll invest very little time and expect a high return
on my investment.

When did forever become a memory of the past?
People come and go.
Strangers have a strange tendency of becoming
familiar.
Deja vu is karma, the one sure thing to come
around.

The circle of life manifesting itself in Deja's vu.
Self-doubt began to obstruct our judgment.
An inconvenient justification of incompetence.
Cultivating adverse reasoning to illogical
outcomes.
My soul wandered about as it maintained eye
contact with its vessel.
It reached out for me with olive branches of
tranquility.
How abnormal to be in search of yourself.

Can I Live

---⋞⋟---

The truth of the matter lies within our Deja vu.
I'm not scared of losing the world
I'm mostly frightened of losing you.
I'm not worried about letting go.
I'm mostly worried about holding on to the truth.

Every soul and every check has a mate.
In our game of tug of war, I'll never reach out,
but I will always surrender to you in open arms.

If we don't argue.
There's nothing wrong.
If we don't hide.
We have nothing to seek.
If we don't endure.
We will never endure.

Do as you please if it pleases you.
How I feel will forever be felt.
There is no resolve that can impede my feelings.
My feelings are absolute; therefore, they are
refined.
I'm always pleased if it pleases you.

No eminent domain could hinder our natural
selection.
I can see past our differences,
yet I'll never mature past the nature of our Deja vu.

So, when you read this, and you know it to be
true.
The truth of the matter is that I was born of
anarchy's sin,
until I was reborn in the baptism of you.

ORIGINS

If you were presented with the answer to life
would it impress you
or would you have more questions?
Let's find the truth while in rotation.
Earth, water, fire, ether, the elements of our
creation.
Find your spectrum on the timeline of truth.
Human nature, life's Deja vu.

Did you know Earth is just where we live, not
where we are from?
A planet where the most intellectual of its species
are the ones who cause the most pollution.
Constant exploration to find a more sustainable
planet as our own.
Why do we search for something new if something
old isn't broken?
An unstable network of natural disasters.
Seemingly its only purpose is catastrophe to its
inhabitants.
Mother Earth, are you alive and if so, are you
well?

Realize that time is only relative to human existence.
Without humans, there would be no need for a timeline.
The earth will still rotate and cultivate its landscape with or without mankind.
So just be, let your truth be lived and outlive death.

DISPROPORTIONATE

The truth sounds so appeasing.
An appetizer to what is yet to come.
The prelude to the rapture.
My appetite created the means to an end.
Fact or fiction, hors d'oeuvres to our omega.
Carnivore thoughts let the meal begin.

An entree comprised of the most unlikely of
ingredients.
A full course meal bound to your satisfaction.
Lost in the garden of Eden,
was this the foundation toward our evolution?
Prepared medium well.
An apple filled with knowledge, the birth of a
revolution.

My sweetest love,
human nature life's Deja vu.
As you digest the meal,
can you understand the essence of time?
What's the alternative to real?
I saved the best for last.
When the desert is meant to appeal?

Rewind to the reservations.
I made plans for two.
Outlined in the blue prints to poetic serenity.
The longer I walk, your footprints start to fade.
Life predicated this moment of clarity.
Human nature casually created
a dinner party in solitude.

FOREVER YOUNG

Memories recollected as words.
A relentless pain with no end in sight.
You've become accustomed to the thin line
between agony and serenity.
Raw emotions feed into the shallowness of your
soul.
Assimilation abandons the prospect of
individuality.
Shun your limits and open your consciousness to
your soul.

A wise premonition once showed me the anti-life
equation.
The answers to my life's work.
Life's complicity in the flash of eve.
So, I began to write the truth yet to be lived.
The ability to forge words that reach as wide as
the ocean.
But nothing can substitute experience.

I seek wisdom while I still exhibit hope.
Natural remedies that are addictive as their vices
I see a coming of age.
One that respects the quality in a puerile being.
May I live internally in this state of mind
The immortal architecture to your reality.

BLACK WIDOW

———◦⟨⟩◦———

A devil in heels, soles of red hue.
Words become our means to an end.
Welcome to my Deja vu.
The flawless essence in all black.
My alpha and omega began and ended with you.
A picture-perfect silhouette.
Life and death's rendezvous.
Though you may come and go,
with every step in your heels,
The path stained with blood
will always lead me back to you.

Beauty dressed down to your birthday suit.
Your words tell me by any means necessary.
A once in a lifetime Deja vu.
Each stride complimenting the next.
In death, your essence is what I look forward to.
A soul so pure, the epitome of serenity.
The pendulum swings as I await our rendezvous.
Your presence balances the scale of truth and
reality.
My lady liberty, your flame becomes my beacon of
hope.
Backdated memories of our past, present, and
the future too.
Lost in the sands of time,
our history will always lead me back to you.

The Eternal Inquiry

What discipline must I pursue in order to
rationalize the sporadic intervals?
My current state of mind has become discontent
with complacency.
Once upon a time I exuberated thought provoking
rhetoric.
Assets and liabilities lie within one's ability to
assess life's intent.
Contemplation assisted my mind in its quest to
comprehend time.
I ponder my capability to emerge triumph over
this deterrent.

Carved from a bias point of view.
Hieroglyphics left as renditions of our past.
Two soulmates bound to an endless Deja vu.
The closer I get to life's anti-equation.
The closer I get to the origin of you.

There's a sculpture that sits in solitude along the
countryside.
Engraved in its cornerstone are the clues of
evidence.
An odyssey in absence of a guide.
I searched for the sculpture in search of our
inheritance.

Though these words were written without ink.
They represented a timeline of uncertainty.
Manifested by humanity's disposition to the
unknown.
Let us always cherish the words of this trilogy.

ORAL AGREEMENT

A blood oath to the words yet to be spoken.
Speak your truth as you begin to confide.
I lost my balance to a silly defect called pride.
When I mentioned renditions of our past
promises,
short term memory started to take its toll.
Words said in the moment meant to withstand
time.
Only to be lived briefly just as they had been said.
Through sickness and health.
Unbeknown to me that didn't cover wealth.
For rich or poor.
Your words seemed priceless.
To stand by my side, to have and to hold.
Where we laid our burdens,
wasn't where we rested our souls.
I replayed your words on repeat.
Countless moments analyzing the tone in your
speech.
Deaf ears to what I wanted to hear.
Balancing the scale of truth.
The next time we converse let our tongues speak
rhetoric that validates our covenant.

Ill Informed

————⋅◈⋅————

You see the world through the eyes of the
conqueror.
Who would ever question the order that allows for
them to thrive in society?
We only have knowledge of what has been
discovered.
Reputable sources from our past.
Yet they had no reference to future normality's.
We tend to explore the unknown in search of
truth.
Who named the universe or is that humanity's
point of view?
What if the world is flat and the skies have no
roof?
Collective bargaining brought us to the concept of
a planet suspended in space.
Do we look out into time or up to the sky?
What if death was just a figment of our
imagination?
The concept of not being able to live.
What's the purpose of free will, if forever isn't a
course of action?

Enlightenment

Knowledge is power, watch me birth a
renaissance off a whim.
My flow is starting to become godly.
I wonder if I keep rhyming the truth,
will the powers to be silence the voice of serenity.
I've seen death followed by suicide, and then
resurrected as soul literacy.
The matrix to my intelligent quotient.
Poetry, you were my first love, I shed tears for
your soul.
That bestowed an immortal agony that stimulated
this poetic irony.
I was never created to be whole.
I dream in black and white, but inception always
takes in consideration of reality.
A life full of sin, may I be demanded to hell.
The life of a Samaritan may heaven welcome me.
Either way, may our souls rest in peace, poetry I
wish you well.

Public Service Announcement

Pardon me while I reintroduce myself.
I know we just met,
but the world is my playground
And my mind, the swing set.

Pardon me while I refinance my prosperity.
I know we just met,
but the world is my consumer.
And my mind, the supplier.

Pardon me while I reinstate my stature.
I know we just met,
But the world is my ceiling.
And my mind, is the most prominent.

Pardon me while I readjust my view.
I know we just met,
But the world is my canvas.
And my mind, the masterpiece.

Pardon me while I reestablish my sanity.
I know we just met,
But the world is my uncertainty.
And my mind, is the truth.

THE FINE PRINT

The right of freedom and liberty.
Only to be sentenced to life imprisonment.
The right of Freedom of speech.
Only to be silenced by those who don't share the
same perception.
The right to bear arms.
Only to be killed and carried by a pallbearer.
The right to a Pursuit of Happiness.
Only to find the pain while chasing uncertainty.
To right to be taxed in exchange for
representation.
Only to be misrepresented by those who cater to
self-interest.
The right to be treated equally regardless of
character.
Only to be judged by your hue.
The right to trial by jury.
Only to be convicted of sins to be forgiven.
The right to protest and assemble.
Only to be jailed by the opposition.
The right to remain silent.
Only to be stripped of your voice.
The only rights I offer you,
is to this endless Deja vu.
I'm writing because writing saved me.
I put the pen to the paper.
Only because my words understand deception.
It's our right to the truth.
Healing through writing,
even human nature isn't foolproof.

TREASON

———◁◈▷———

I must admit, I've always needed you to be my
peripheral.
To see the things that I can't see through.
I wanted a life alone in solitude.
A tunnel vision steadfast toward my dreams.
But a premonition showed me the dangerous
unforeseen.

No weapon formed against us shall prosper,
but the fall of Troy did come from a gift and a
curse.
A bond that transcends time.
Your absence hinders progress.
For every action, you're the reaction.
One without the other, soul mates destined to
forsake.

History shows us most empires fall from within.
Become the eyes in the back of my head.
Brutus, Guy, Ephialtes, Judas, e tu?
Betrayal by the ones who sit at our table,
and by the ones who stand by our side.
A betrayal in the form of mutiny, never to be
foreseen.
A traitor never has to hide.
In plain view, our downfall waits for our demise.

In Theory

Like the truth left astray,
I believed in human nature.
I turned the hourglass sideways.
Time stood still, an endless Deja vu.
I gazed out onto the stars
as they gazed back at you.

Soon,
I'll distance myself from my history.
Fact or fiction distinguish between the two.
Words of wisdom left construed by his story.
Heavy burdens that leave no clue.

The thin line between content
and contemplate as I weigh my options.
What constitutes my perception?
Is my reasoning valid or measured?

Signs carved into hieroglyphics
and the city beneath the sea.
The edge of earth or an ocean with no beginning.
They tell a story still unbeknown to modern
times.
Discoveries still undiscovered.
I place my pen to paper, the narrator to mankind

FREE WILL

———◦◆◦———

I am alone in search of my half.
I feel obligated to my reader's burdens.
All that brings tears to my eyes.
They had no defense at the time they needed.

What makes this so different from the rest?
If a man looks in the mirror will he see his
mistress
or the clarity of the glass?
Is he held responsible for the work of the world?
His need for flesh and bone.
To feed his furnace, his will of fire.
What becomes of a man whose fire is burnt out?

You claim to be true and to be free,
but the truth inside is blinding to sovereignty.
When his patience passes by a living breath,
he wishes to have one of his own.
Does he buy, sell, trade, steal or kill?

Hiding the sorrows of humanity.
This is not freedom.
I came with no burden of my own.
I was a man of love not of war.
Yet I became collateral damage in search of the
truth.

Ulterior Motives

What becomes of an endless rhyme?
When I only wrote to relive a timeless Deja vu.
How do I exist outside the literacy of our soul?
Where I no longer write to you?
When the lonely nights came,
I just wanted you to leave me alone.
Codependency didn't come with a receipt,
And its only exchange was solitude.

I couldn't alter your way of thinking
so, I began to write down my deception.
My attempt to validate my well-being.
A poetic approach to unforeseen rhetoric.

I inquired about the intent of our emotions.
Yet you replied with questions
you had already answered internally.
Did deja vu ever consider that I was one step
ahead of you?

As my words transformed an uncandid situation.
You became infatuated with my reflection.
As I rained fire, stanzas became our precipitation.
You became fascinated with my perception.

We learned to think before we learned to write.
So, even though our words were legible, they were
illiterate too.

Before I give the past back to the present's future.
I think of my presence in a time related to you.
Before I contemplate solitude,
I think of us in a time related to Deja vu.
Soul mates, neither divided or multiplied by two.

Rest in Peace

I'm an artist, you will be my piece.
And like the greats before me
my works of art shall be rereleased.
Overtime they will surely come to understand.
Like modern and surreal, a renaissance to your
will.
I will not stay within your prism, your prison of
the understood.

No sympathy for those trying to sleep in.
Sympathy is a thing of the past, present, and
future.
It's captivating to spread your ashes
beneath the feet of the ones you adored.
To know they are in pain and
that you meaningfully caused it.
Cause and effect intertwined with the time of fate.

I wrote down my truth,
as a present that transcends death.
Sentenced to a life of awaiting fate.
I've come this far just to be buried and replaced.
I look on with innocence.
I find comfort in saving grace.
I like to watch that history fade,
as time realizes there's no escape.

Coming of Age

As a poet, I have a desire to create.
As a human, I aspire to relate.
Poetry, you are my truth.
In my pursuit of happiness,
I place all my burdens on you.

A society that thrives on your ability to produce.
For the common good, law and order to the
misunderstood.
Technological advances designated toward the
future.
The future is here what's your contribution to
history?
Will your name be carved into presents past?
Or is your presence just arbitrary?

As I balance the scales of our alternative realities.
For a moment, I begin to release.
I begin to understand what it means to be a part
of society.
Commerce constructed to provide the means to
the pursuit of happiness.
One nation devised for the common good.

Play your role, now your role.
Is this a right or a privilege?
Poetry you are my shelter.
No opposition can phase this Deja vu,
Be the sole proprietor of my free will.

The Habitual Tendency

———⬦⬦———

I get in the habit of searching for answers with no
questions.
An empathetic approach to understanding what
is meant to be understood.
I forget that I lacked empathy, so I approached
from a scientific perspective.
I get in the habit of researching my truth.
A strategic approach that encompasses the
mental, spiritual and physical constructs of
nature.
I forget that alternatives exist to every truth.
I get in the habit of formulating hypotheses
around questions to answers.
A sympathetic approach that aims to present
an argument where discussion is an intangible
asset.
I forget that whether my prediction is accurate,
the method is consistent.
I get in the habit of experimenting with the truth.
An unrealistic approach to understanding the
variables that affect each outcome.
I forget frequency is the one true variable that
verifies the truth.
I get in the habit of drawing conclusions where
there should be an analyst.
An optimistic approach to a concrete solution.
I remember that this is all just a Deja vu.

HALLUCINATE

———◈◈———

I remembered when the feelings were so deep.
It was your style and it was your grace.
I could feel you in my sleep.
The sensuality behind serenity.
Hooked on your phonics.
Word play was my form of foreplay.
A climax that blended into every rhyme.
Daydreaming of that lustful Deja vu.
Lust in the form of passion.
Time after time thinking of you.

Did I wake up to your reality?
Did you have the answers?
Questions that question my memory.
I didn't mean to tell the truth.
I only sought a reaction to your perception.
Occasionally, I lied because I was confused.
I didn't mean to deceive your perception.
I'm aware at times that I'm lost in translation.
To my recollection,
the events prior to this are misconstrued.
A selective memory in which I leave room
deception.

THEORETICAL PAST AGGRESSIONS

Like the truth in the mirror
I believed in human nature.
I gazed out onto the stars
as they gazed back at you.

I buried the hourglass sideways.
Time stood still, an endless Deja vu.
The truth behind humanity left without a clue.
Words of Wise left construed by his story.
Fact or fiction let me hypothesize the variance
between the two.

Signs carved into hieroglyphics and the city
beneath the sea.
The edge of earth or an ocean with no beginning.
They tell a story still unbeknown to modern
times.
Discoveries still undiscovered.
Pen and paper, the new manipulator of mankind.

INVOLUNTARY

A timeless flow that will always watch you come
and go.
My worth was that of rain over a waterfall.
Long before this Deja vu,
I was already flowing toward our downfall.
I lay alone in a city that never sleeps.
It's difficult to look past our past to see our story
had history.
When I fell back, you realized you had nothing to
fall back on.
Fate willed or to be or not to be.
In solitude, I'll hide while you seek.
You're a mismatch to my ambition.
You could never set fire to the rain
that weathered my blurred vision.
Maturity gifted with wisdom.
I'm the author of our religion.

LUCIFER'S SONATA

A heart-broken angel
The piercing sound of an angel's melody
Exalting his voice against the most high
His choir sings in agony
Hear their cries as they lust for life
Filled with pride, discontent and jealousy
A heart unhinged
Full of wisdom and everlasting beauty
The devil may cry in the end
A lust for life his only imperfection
An immortal sinner bound to righteousness
A heart damned to hell
He comes bearing gifts, the anti-equation to life
Life's forbidden fruit nurtured in the garden of
eve
More sensual than a siren's appeal
His lust for life renders you defenseless to his will
A heart driven by deception
A rebellion against creation
The ability to sway the hearts of man
He comes in the form of prophecy
All to free the sanity of your free will

ZION

It was my home
You were my reality
The lies behind my fears
My utopia, the unspoken truth.
A dream that couldn't last,
My heritage, the genetic oracle.
The reincarnation of reality
The annunciation of love
It was my shelter
You were my sanity
A rainbow before the storm
My paradise, the spoken word
A nightmare always meant to be
The epitome of love
The creation of reality
It was my asylum
You were my chivalry
A place to lay my head
The end to nomadic lust
Now I rest under the fire of a bridge
As I slumber in solitude
Vagrancy was my home

SOLICITATION

My demeanor was self-righteous.
Down to its stubborn perception.
In lieu of my suffering, poetry blessed me.
The blueprints to the embodiment of
imperfection.

I took notice of everything I despised about the
makeup of my anatomy.
The anticipation to the answers of the unknown.
A sense of appeal that transcends time.

Inviting reasoning to life's misunderstandings.
The sands of time reaching out its hands.
Evolution inspired by fear.
I grow weary to which I do not understand.
As the end times draw near.
What truth keeps you sane?

I lay alone in a city that never sleeps.
It's difficult to look past our past to see our story
had history.
When I fell back, you realized you had nothing to
fall back on.
Fate willed us to be or not to be.

Our calm before the storm.
A timeless flow that will always watch you come
and go.

My worth was that of rain over a waterfall.
Long before this Deja vu.
I was already flowing toward our downfall.

In solitude, I'll hide while you seek.
You're a mismatch to my ambition.
You could never set fire to the rain
that weather my blurred vision.
Maturity gifted with wisdom.
I'm the author of our religion.

GUILTY CONSCIENCE

———— ❖ ————

Only the beautiful wonder about their inner
appearance.
I'm shallow, but what feelings aren't deep.
I was an adolescent
You made me abnormal.
Maturity taught me sex appeal
Knowing my life expectancy,
I began to ponder my sanity.
The anticipation of answers to the unresolved.
Evolution inspired by fear.
Inviting reasoning and understanding.
A sense of pride that transcends time.

Until it's beautiful,
I wanted my last time to be with you.
Knowing that the feeling would be the first.
Even though I had met you before.
In my dreams you said hello.
However, when I awoke,
I realized your goodbye had become my sleeping
willow.
I just wanted to be your ventriloquist,
so, I can hear the words I never heard.
As I cherished your warmth as you pulled me
closer.
Knowing that I wouldn't be immune to your cold
shoulder.
The death clause justified every moment we spent
together

Serial Lust

If you're a star, I'm your creative space.
I can't manipulate your fate.
I won't ever impede on who you're meant to be.
I may not always agree with your outcome.
However, I'll always want to be with the person
you have become.
Everything I love about you, me too.
I'm addicted to your affection.
My thoughts become illiterate around you.
Your smile is my fantasy.
I adore your integrity.
My essence is seeping out.
Your aroma is my therapy.
My addictions reek of your soul.
Your touch warms my integrity.
I day dream about you when my dreams don't
come true.
Even as an obstacle, I will always bend to your
will.
I yearn for our Deja vu.

Mind Control

How could you ever relate, you were never the
intended audience?
You don't have the intellect to comprehend my
worth.
Your point of view is flawed because you aren't.
Do you ever find yourself speaking out loud to
someone
who used to be by your side only to be met with
an echo?
Do you ever find yourself writing to the one,
the muse behind your art, knowing they would
never respond?

I had to learn that the world doesn't end when
you can't find your means to an end.
Focused on lust and material gain.
My burdens weighed heavy on stepping stones.
While logic kept me in place,
Their incompetence blundered the truth.
The current me is content with I.
I was overzealous to approach life with common
sense.
In hindsight, solitude was the only way we would
see eye to eye.

OPEN BORDERS

————◆◈◆————

I'll casually take you to a Utopia.
Imagine a world where a smile is a common grin.
Where your subconscious releases you from your
coma.
A world with no borders and no sin.
Where love and peace are the qualities that stand
out.

When did war, conformity, and poverty define
humanity?
Refugees seeking the humility of your faith.
Driven from their homes they seek refuge.
It bothers me how we are quick to provide food
and shelter
to household animals in need of relief.
But are quick to turn away humans because of
their beliefs.

Freedom of speech comes with free will.
Open your door to those who differ from you.
Yes, they may share a different belief,
but they also share a common ancestry.
Open your borders to the vagrants you created.
Show empathy and care not because they value
your faith,
but because every faith is founded on civility.

INTELLIGENCE QUOTIENT

Wisdom comes from time spent on earth.
Yet intellect is decided while puerility is still in
effect.
Common sense, life's priceless commodity.
A free world that ranks 17th in intellect.
Yet 1st in nuclear capabilities.
Why educate your society when war has a higher
probability?
Why do we constantly categorize stupidity?
Standardized test that determines your worth.
Does your child have a learning disability?
Or is the curriculum formulated in a flawed
society?
Gifted retarded, the label bestowed upon me.
Bunched into a group of likeminded individuals.
The gifted separated from the masses.
All bestowed with various forms of
understanding.
The truth behind critical thinking
is that it lacks the basic principles of selective
reasoning.

DUE PROCESS

In a country founded on their sins being forgiven,
are there any crimes that equals execution?
An eye for an eye.
The ability to be stoned to death due to religious
persecution.
Petty crimes committed with sentences
designated for treason.
Did the punishment fit the crime?
It is your right to be jailed
and to be treated as an animal?
Who but the wealthy could make bail?
Institutionalization, private interest's dependence.
The inhumane reality of justice.
Rehabilitation, the wealthier life sentence.
A trial by jury selected not by coincidence,
but strategically in lieu of your defense.
Imagine if injustice was made illegal.
A society in desperate need of reform.
We the people, by the people, for the people.

Standard Deviation

———————◆◆◆———————

Always walk by my side
And let the rest follow in our footsteps.
A small circle enables prosperity to flourish from
within.
Beauty amid the mist of imperfection.
In search of a common intellect to make sense.
The veil of peace cloaks itself in loneliness.
Knowledge can force you into solitude.
Wisdom will keep you there.
My first impressions are shallow.
I let time fill in the blanks.
A cautious approach to your salutation.

My truth lies within the skin I am in.
A constant state of mind.
Mortal injuries that outlive mortality.
How I wish to see the truth of the world without
pain.
My perception lacks empathy.
Beneath the surface lies agony.
No medical relief to remedy this situation.
Natural remedies come in the form of addiction.
A pain never meant to subside, a life in agony,
death will be the cure to my affliction.

The ink in my imagery pen felt empty.
I woke to more thoughts than words.
No quality in the quantity.

Where's the voice to emotional reasoning?
My soul refuses to see the imperfection of our
reality.
I woke to a lackluster of emotional stimulation.
This isn't poetry, this is deviation.
It's the fire catching up to our damnation.
The bond that soul mates share.
The perfection of imperfection
Truth is the lust that hinders care.

CONTINUUM

The deception of time lies within the history of
humanity.
Dating back to archaic times,
did we manifest the alpha and the omega?
Was the creation of a beginning and an end...?
man's need for past present and future?
Does the future receive the news late?
Are the time zones ahead of our time or behind
the times we live in?
Historians debate the timeline of our existence.
While scientist hypothesis on the inevitability of
our extinction.

You've come and gone countless times over time.
So, your goodbyes are abnormal.
You became my religion.
Something I could believe in but would steadily
test my faith.
I'm just worried what I'll become without you.
A soul forced to solidarity.
I'm worried that I won't be here when you need
me, like when I needed you.
Thus, creating an endless Deja vu.
I'm not good with words, but what's the point of
speaking,
if you don't believe the one fated to hear you.

I should be dead.
Don't fall privy to the deceit.
Truth will always be defined by
peace and prosperity.
Even when they put words in your mouth,
Silence is ...and will always be golden.
I tried to camouflage the pain.
But my sanity was taken before eighteen.
I remember gracing life with my knees.
Pleading to the god that I believed in to spare my
agony.
However, I didn't awake to serenity.
Ever since then I turned my back hope and
focused on reality.

DICTUM

Parables, humanity's faith in ancient writings.
Never look a gift horse in the mouth,
Symbolism giving intangibles tangibility
What doesn't kill you makes you stronger.
Metaphors meant to enlighten.
Sayings designed to deter.
What goes around comes around.
Sayings meant to guide.
Life's golden rule.
Do unto others as they would do unto you.
The sinner man's prayer.
People come and go,
Death and taxes, the only guarantees.
When will we speak our truth?

When will enough become the reason for change?
Our animal instinct to wage war.
The manifesto to our destiny.
Crimes committed under the veil of freedom.
Nuclear times spell natural disasters.
The war on drugs waged by its supplier.
Guns, man's only weapon against the beast he
cannot tame.

Religious adversaries waging war on a what if.
Killings in the name of a higher power.
Destruction stemmed from mutual hate
with the human population as its collateral
damage.
How many innocents' lives must perish before
our eyes
before profit is regarded as less than humanity?
The words of a few affect the mortality of the
many.
Men and women who laid down their lives for
peace and honor.
I pray that your leaders speak of peace and
stability.

DEAD ON ARRIVAL

Prejudice hinders love.
A blind soul is deaf to its heartbeat.
Black and white, views of the colorblind.
When you see me,
you won't notice me because of how I see you.

I'm not lost.
Time heals all.
I turned the hourglass sideways, time stood still.
Standing still, while the world rotates around me.
It means I'm just taking it all in.
Becoming the foundation on which self-worth
stands on.

Pride breeds regret.
I was a fool to not spend my last moments with
you.
I'm lost on how to start over without you.
Your perfection can never be duplicated.
However, these words will place hold our Deja vu.

I'm no god, I am no idol.
I lost my balance in search of truth.
I'm the overture to Deja vu.
Living out the reoccurrence of ignorance that I'm
exposed to.
I just drink to forgive.
You will never comprehend my insanity.

My knowledge is vast, but my past is
misconstrued.
Just realize that healing through writing is the
only truth into which I console.

Articulate

The voice of the mute soul.
All I have are leftover words.
I don't feel the emotions behind them.
Do writers ever receive love notes or just the
experience to create them?
I rolled the dice and solitude bounced back.
One without the other to have and to hold.
What's the difference between a heartbreak and a
heart attack?
Life, the muse to an agony untold.
Look back at the collateral damage in his history.
Where were you during the midst of his
contemplation?
A writing community that lacks poetic serenity.
Manipulation for substance in the form of a
charitable donation.

I was lost.
Thinking of you, I wanted to reach out.
But pain is internal and words can only travel so
far.
Just because we aren't holding hands, doesn't
mean we're not together.
Just because we are together, doesn't mean I
belong to you.
I'm the coldest memory of the summer.
When you see me, remember that soul literacy
wasn't born of petulance.

I'm the enigma to your common sense.
The ordained introvert to your presence.
In essence, I'll be what reality and fate meant for
us to be.
Hopefully that doesn't come with a return policy.

REOCCURRENCE

———— ⋖❖⋗ ————

Even with a roof over your head, you still search
for a home.
The nomads fall into lust.
Even with a twenty-twenty view,
treason is overlooked.
The romantic's love is just.
Even with blueprints,
the rest only discover what their souls were
meant to find.

To never ever experience the joy of their laughter
again.
The thought of them will still merit a smile.
Their care will always be remembered as a
butterfly's cocoon.
Never knowing how much their existence meant
to you.
Only knowing their beauty after their bloom.

It would never be the same, and that's when they
became indifferent.
Who were we ever truly if fate willed us to be
strangers in the end?
Be real with me and tell me the truth or else I'll
never know the lie within myself.
A feeling that would always seem familiar, yet
foreign to my senses.

Tell me the truth, were you ever real with me.
Was your final judgement fair when fate hung our
jury?
Souls that only belonged to our kind.
Bound to an endless Deja vu, karma becomes
necessary.
Souls that only belonged to our kind.
Bound to an endless Deja vu, karma becomes
necessary.

TRIVIAL

—————⟨⊱⊰⟩—————

The reality of the inception in our dreams was to
confront the truth with facts.
While we argued libel in lieu of our self-inflicted
lust for love.
The genetic makeup of our reality
was to be the blueprint of soulmates.
While we contemplated thought provoking
theories in lieu of our self-perceived lust for life.

With me there was nothing to prove;
however, I knew you would always conform to
their expectations.
A gentleman bound to chivalry.
I wonder...would you join the conversation of
those living bi-curiously through you.

Masculinity was beneath you, as you held me in
your truth.
Alone with you, I experienced the unhinged and
the unknown.
All the while you swayed public opinion by
tethering the truth.
I just wanted your emotions.
They would always know the personified you.
So, I fell back, and you had nothing to fall back on.
I saw through the absence of time.
Forward progress was the antonym to me and
you.

I took a step back just to watch your back.
Premature premonitions turned out to be our
Deja vu.

Subpoenaed

The afterlife calls you home.
Your time has come in this reality.
The final judgement to your truth.
As you begin to replay your history,
do you begin to recall your sins or your good
deeds?
The final judgment to decide your fate.
The trial of your lifetime.
Your lawyer reads your autobiography aloud.
The literature to your truth.
Think ahead to this reality.
Ask yourself is the current you worth the mercy
of your peers.
or have you lived to be the author of your
everlasting suffering?

OPEN LETTER

---⋅◈⋅---

Dear, number two.

Pen in hand as I write to you again.
Pencils meant to erase.
I was lying to you when I told the truth.
The truth was in my ink.
A permanent pen seal to the truth.
Each letter sharpening our bond.
We were pen pals bound to yours truly.
As our pendulum began to rhyme,
The sands of time found our love to be unruly.
Once dependent on your response.
Now my letters fall on death ears, un-penciling
our reality.
I've now found serenity in solitude.
From me to you.
Writing only to become independent of
dependency.

Sincerely, Deja vu.

MY SOULMATES PRAYER

Say what you will, but I pray my soul to keep.
A moonless night...
Where darkness hides in the shade.
Attempting to analyze your will to leave me
bested.
Was all this just a Deja vu?
Mere moments keep me wondering,
are you going to die without saying hello again?
Or was your goodbye a means to an end?
Are you done with keeping me abide in my sin?
Or has my suffering only yet begun to begin?

My favorite poem is the one where I would write
your name over and over again
Not out of love, but to sketch our history
You used to tell me that I was crazy and
abnormal beyond belief.
I would listen, but it wasn't until your departure
that I heard your pleas.
I moved away to put distance between insanity.
I just didn't factor the mental strain it would put
on my sanity.

The cache to his history.
My chords will become the harmony to our poetic
serenity.
Thoughts become words unknowingly, as a writer
gazed upon his canvas.

I have enough memories of our love to paint a
masterpiece from memory.
A blank canvas comes to life as he attempts to
recreate a Deja vu.
A painter, poet, and musician, the trilogy to his
legacy.

BURN AFTER READING

Two poets in love was nothing short of opposition
research.
We always reached out, so we never felt the need
to hold on.
We would write to each other out of love not
knowing our words would become our SOS.
I would lust seeking a Deja vu that would lead to
our rendezvous.
You knew our souls were meant yet you allowed
me to stray in contempt.
I would always say forever would never be
enough.
You saw your history in me that's why you saw
past me.
I used to come and go, but in the end karma
stayed.
You ignored my words, but always knew my
thoughts.
With all that makeup on how was I supposed to
be real with you?
All the while you made up the truth.
Be real with you and maybe we can make up the
time I wasn't real with you
I'm beyond the imagination of me.
I wasn't sober when I said I loved, but I was
drunk when I fell in love with you.
Writing with no muse is an endless Deja vu.
There's only a from, no to.

Aroma Therapy

A deep breath can hinder your release.
Tapped into my thoughts
my soul starts to rest in peace.
My mind seemingly begins to rhyme.
It's not until I regain focus
that I begin to contemplate time.
Stimulating words bound to context.
The essence of intuitive writing
taking on the form of subjects.
Releasing the constraints that bind my mind.
A vision that becomes so clear.
The closer I come to a perfect scene.
As I show you this rhyme is far from near.
A gift bestowed by a perfect being.
A prelude to a monologue.
Timing each rhyme to cater to the next.
Mental phrases being used to stimulate.
Somewhat divisive, always taking out of context.
A rhyme scheme meant to manipulate.
To write while I contemplate pain.
Towards the end of this perfect scene
my conscious I began to regain.
The prelude to the perfect rhyme scheme
To think it all began with one breath.
Thoughts written in my pastime,
words written to outlive death
meant to last a lifetime.
Words written arbitrarily.
Such a simple concept, an endless rhyme.
One might overlook that this is my therapy.

AU REVOIR

I would have rather been the rock of your
foundation than your mountain's peak.
You just got lost trying to find yourself.
I am a blessing that will not be received until I'm
gone.
You shouldn't have played mind games unless
you were willing to lose yourself.
I was once the parasite; I was once the host.
If you only knew what you've been told, were you
ever truly self-aware?
A symbiotic approach to fate, that's our free will.
You and I became someone we didn't used to be,
the people we were meant to be.

This too has come to an end.
Maybe one day I'll write to you again.
A point in time where I am beyond the
imagination of me.
This was my natural appeal to your mind, body,
and soul.
The day of reckoning to my
philosophical approach.
A term all too familiar to you, Healing through
writing.

An endless rhyme that told the story of a
beautiful Deja vu.
It pains me to walk away from my therapy,
but I become infatuated with this new-found
serenity.
I hope these words act as a guide as a reminder
that we are one in the same.
Thank you for the humility you've shown me
through empathy.
Maybe one, maybe two, maybe three.
There will come a day when I return with the
wisdom to write the conscious that heals society.

A WRITER'S QUARREL

Deep within the poetry community,
there's a writer that thrives in solidarity.
Questions arise as my burdens begin to weigh.
What constitutes my perception?
The thin line between content and contemplate.
Is my reasoning valid or is it measured?
I have a way with words,
but what distinguishes me from their poetry?
This is my passion; I seek no fame.
If I didn't hold back would I become subject to
scrutiny?
Doubt shrouds the essence of healing through
writing.
I see growth with no place to grow.
This is more than writers block.
A poetic pilgrim, the metamorphosis I must
undergo.

BIO

Larry Foster is a graduate of Johnson Wales University. He also is the author of *The Blueprints to a Black Heart.*

Visit www.Souliteracy.com

SouLiteracy

www.ingramcontent.com/pod-product-compliance
Lightning Source LLC
Chambersburg PA
CBHW031602110426
42742CB00036B/661